A TALE OF HANSEL AND GRETEL

NIBBLE NIBBLE MOUSEKIN

JOAN WALSH ANGLUND

HARCOURT, BRACE & WORLD, INC., NEW YORK

by the same author

A FRIEND IS SOMEONE WHO LIKES YOU

THE BRAVE COWBOY

LOOK OUT THE WINDOW

LOVE IS A SPECIAL WAY OF FEELING

IN A PUMPKIN SHELL

COWBOY AND HIS FRIEND

CHRISTMAS IS A TIME OF GIVING

A STORY BY THE BROTHERS GRIMM

Library of Congress Catalog Card Number: 62-14422
Printed in the United States of America

For my father,
Tom Walsh

ONCE upon a time, on the edge of a deep, dark forest, there lived a poor woodcutter with his wife and his two children, Hansel and Gretel. Times were hard for the woodcutter, and often there was little in the house to eat.

One night when he lay in bed, the poor man sighed and said to his wife, "What will become of us? The potatoes are eaten, the bread is almost gone, and the cupboard will soon be bare. How can we feed our poor children?"

But his wife, who was not the children's real mother, was a hardhearted woman. She didn't care what became of Hansel and Gretel. And to herself she thought, "If only there were not four mouths to feed, then the woodcutter and I would do very well. What a good plan it would be to lead the children into the woods and leave them there." But she did not speak of her schemes. Instead she answered her husband sweetly: "I have heard that in the forest the wild berries are ripe. Tomorrow we shall all go to gather some. Then the dear children will not go hungry."

Now Hansel and Gretel had heard all that their parents had said. Hansel did not trust his selfish stepmother, and so early the next morning, before anyone else was awake, he slipped from the house and filled his pockets with round white pebbles. Soon the family was ready, and they set off through the forest in search of berries.

When they came into the deepest part of the forest, the wife cleverly said, "We will find more berries if we search in different places. We will go this way, and you, Hansel and Gretel, go that." And she pointed to where the forest looked even darker and the underbrush thicker and more tangled.

The children did as they were told and began filling their baskets with ripe red berries. They were so busy, they didn't realize how late it was and how silent the forest had become. Now as they looked about them, they saw that the sun had set, the birds were hushed, and all about them was dim gray twilight.

"Oh, Hansel," said Gretel. "It is getting so dark, and I do not see our father and mother. We are lost."

"Don't be afraid, Gretel. As we walked along, I dropped white pebbles. Just wait until the moon comes out, and I shall find the way home."

Soon the moon did rise. It shone on the white pebbles and made them glitter in the darkness. With the bright pebbles to guide them, the children found their way back easily.

And when they reached home, their father, who had been searching everywhere for them, hugged them in his big strong arms. But their stepmother looked crosser than ever.

And to herself she thought, "Tomorrow I shall take them even farther into the forest. And this time, they won't find their way out."

The following day they all started out to pick berries once again. This time, Hansel had not gathered pebbles, but he dropped bread crumbs behind him instead.

Once again, when they were in the deepest part of the forest, the sly stepmother said, "Your father and I will go this way, and you, Hansel and Gretel, go that." And she pointed to where the forest was even darker and the underbrush grew thicker and more tangled.

The two children did as they were told and began filling their baskets with ripe red berries. Once again, they were so busy, they took no notice of the setting sun. Slowly the light faded from the sky and the forest grew still. Suddenly, Gretel stood up. "Oh, Hansel," she said. "It is getting so dark. I do not see our father and mother. Now we are really lost."

"Don't be afraid, Gretel. I scattered bread crumbs along our path. Wait until the moon comes out, and I shall find the way home."

But when they looked for the crumbs, they could not find any at all, for the many small birds that lived in the woods had eaten every one. Poor Gretel began to cry.

Hansel put his arm around his little sister. On and on they wandered, and the farther they went, the deeper they lost themselves in the thick black forest.

At last they could go no farther, and lying down at the foot of a great tree, the tired children fell fast asleep. Soon it was morning, and refreshed by their sleep, Hansel and Gretel set off once more.

They had wandered most of the day when suddenly in a clearing they came upon a strange little house. The children stopped in amazement, for the cottage was made of gingerbread. Its roof dripped with thick white frosting, and it sparkled with gum drops and peppermint sticks. Its chimney was a cookie, and the windows were clear sugar. To the hungry children it looked delicious.

"Oh!" said Hansel. "Here is something for us! We shall have a good meal." And he ran forward and broke off a little piece of trimming from the house, while Gretel helped herself to a cookie from the roof. Then there was heard a wee little voice from within the cottage.

"Nibble nibble mousekin,
Who's nibbling at my housekin?"

But the children paid no attention. Hansel boldly seized a part of the house itself, and Gretel pulled out a sugar pane from one of the windows. Again the wee little voice came from within the cottage.

"Nibble nibble mousekin,
Who's nibbling at my housekin?"

Still the children didn't listen and went on eating. Then all at once the door opened, and out of the sugary cottage came an ugly old woman. Hansel and Gretel were so surprised, they dropped what they had taken.

But their first fear was soon put to rest, for the old woman said in a voice as sweet as honey:

"Ah, my little dears, who brought you here? Come in and stay a while! Nothing will harm you, and I will feed you sugarplums and candy."

She took them by the hand and, without thinking, they followed her into the house. She set before them a dinner of pancakes and honey, milk, apples, and nuts. Soon Hansel and Gretel were eating so greedily, they forgot to be on their guard against the old woman. After dinner, she showed them two little white beds into which they crept, and there they slept through the night.

Early in the morning, before Hansel and Gretel awoke, the old woman got up, and looking at the children greedily, she murmured, "Sweet little dears, they will be dainty morsels."

For this old woman, who pretended to be so sweet and kind, was really a mean and crafty old witch who had built that sweet, sugary cottage on purpose to catch little children and pop them into her oven and make a grand feast of them.

The wicked witch yanked Hansel out of bed with one bony hand and dragged him off to a cage. There she locked him up and left him, although he shook the bars and screamed loudly to be let out. Then she came back and shook Gretel roughly. "Get up, little lazybones, and cook something for your brother. He's much too thin, but if we feed him well, what a plump, tasty meal he will make."

When Gretel heard this, she burst into tears, but it did no good. She must do as the witch ordered. And so every day after, Gretel had to fetch the wood, lay the table, and sweep the floor, while Hansel must wait in his cage.

Each day the old woman hobbled to the cage and cried, "Hansel, put out your finger so I can tell how fat you are."

But Hansel had found an old chicken bone in the corner of his cage, and each day he held out the bone instead of his finger. And since the old witch could not see very well, she thought it really was his finger and wondered why he never grew any fatter.

"Drat that boy!" she cried. "He gets thinner every day. But fat or thin, we'll cook him this morning."

The witch built a roaring fire in the oven, and then she said to Gretel, "But first we'll bake the bread. Creep into the oven, little sweetie, and see if it is properly heated. If it is, then we'll put in our loaves." She meant to bang the door shut and have a girl as well as a boy for her breakfast. But by this time Gretel guessed what the old woman intended. So she answered:

"I don't know how to get into the oven."

"Ah, my dear little Sugar Dolly," cried the witch. "Just crawl in. The opening is quite big enough, you can see.... I could even do it myself."

As she spoke, she hobbled up and poked her head into the opening. Quick as a wink, Gretel gave her a shove and sent the wicked witch sprawling, head first, into the oven. Then Gretel banged the door and bolted it, leaving the witch to bake inside.

Quickly Gretel ran to the cage. She opened the door,
and out popped Hansel. "Hansel, we are saved!" she
cried. "The old witch is dead!"

How delighted they were! They kissed each other and
danced about with joy.

Now that they did not have to be afraid of the witch, they looked through her tiny house, and hidden in every corner they found jewels and pearls and gold pieces enough to last a lifetime. Gretel filled her basket full, while Hansel stuffed his pockets with as much as they would hold.

Then the children left the gingerbread house and hurried through the woods as fast as their legs would carry them.

They had not gone far when whom should they see but their father, who had been searching day and night for his lost children. Now he was overjoyed to see them. He held his little ones close and covered them with kisses.

When they were safely home, the woodcutter told them how their stepmother had run away. Frightened by the evil things she had done, she had left the cottage and had never been seen since.

Now with the gold and treasures they had found, the little family need never worry about being poor again. And so, together in their little house, they lived safe and happy forever.